Table of Contents

T0077032

Bridging The Gap Between Middle School and High School

1

Bridging The Gap between Middle School and High School

What DIRECTORS Can Do...

High school and middle school directors must think of themselves as one faculty that works together on a consistent basis to provide one sequential program for each participant.

High school directors can:

- **Partner with middle school directors** to plan a variety of recruitment activities with the elementary school so that the instrumental music program is viewed as a sequential program that concludes with high school graduation.

- **Provide an annual assembly at the elementary school(s) in full regalia.** The high school band can march through the school to an energetic cadence to bring all students into the performance venue and, at some point during the concert, choose an elementary student to conduct the band. This is when students are the most impressionable, and a performance like this will predispose students to playing in the high school program.

- **Attend "Instrument Night" when students are selecting their instruments for the first time.** This works to ensure that parents meet the high school director and see the continuum within the program. Students will subsequently discover a comfort zone of familiarity as they progress from one school to the next.

- **Host a "Marching Band Night" at the high school with the eighth-graders from the middle school(s) featured prominently in the halftime show.** Middle school directors should be involved in the planning and should be invited to conduct in this performance. To ensure their subsequent participation, make this an exceptional and memorable experience that guarantees success for these younger musicians.

- **Work with middle school directors to provide a free "Summer Lesson Program" for beginning students.** Students will become acquainted with the high school director(s) in a more individualized, casual setting right from the very beginning, plus it positions the program as one that continues through high school.

- **Visit the middle school(s) in a variety of contexts to enjoy the product of those programs.** This can include the high school directors providing a clinic for the band, directing sectionals or simply observing rehearsals to get to know the students better. A "thumbs up" from the high school director provides positive reinforcement to the middle school students.

- **Show respect and continuity by attending the middle school concerts (and middle school directors can do the same by attending high school concerts) and encouraging students to do so as well.** Directors should consider offering extra credit for concert attendance. Another very positive example that students take note of is to participate in each other's concerts in some significant way—conducting a selection, emceeing the performance, making presentations, etc. The key is for the high school director to become a familiar face in all aspects of the middle school program and vice versa.

Want more tips for keeping music strong in your schools?
Go to: **www.supportmusic.com**

Produced by the Music Achievement Council

The **Music Achievement Council (MAC)** is an action-oriented nonprofit organization sponsored by the National Association of School Music Dealers (NASMD) and the National Association of Music Merchants (NAMM). MAC is made up of three representatives from NASMD, three manufacturers and suppliers of Instrumental Music products and one representative from NAMM. The group's purpose is to enable more students to begin and stay in instrumental music programs by sharing real-world successful strategies developed by instrumental music teachers. The council was formed in 1983 and reorganized in 1990, forming a nonprofit 501(c)(6) organization.

The Music Achievement Council appreciates the support and guidance of NAMM in the development of these materials.

Music Achievement Council
5790 Armada Drive
Carlsbad, CA 92008
www.musicachievementcouncil.org
info@namm.org

Bridging The Gap between Middle School and High School

Tips For Ensuring A Seamless Music Education Experience

Students continue to participate in our music education programs because they cannot imagine school without the meaningful engagement that our courses provide. Yet, for one reason or another, not all of our students continue their participation throughout their high school years. In fact, it's the transition from middle school to high school that has been identified as being the most crucial period in retaining our students.

The key to successful retention is **ACTION.** On the next pages are a number of strategies that successful instrumental music educators and their constituents use to ensure a seamless transition from the first day that the student picks up their instrument through high school graduation—and beyond.

- **Host the first concert of the year for the advanced ensemble(s) from the middle school(s).** This will demonstrate the sequential development and expectations of the entire program. Because this concert would take place in the high school auditorium, middle school students will easily visualize themselves playing while in high school and parents will visualize their students participating at this level. The directors should work together to provide a finale in which the high school and middle school students perform together.

- **Invite the middle school students to play with the high school pep band and make it fun.** Have the high school students make welcome signs and name tags. Have a little pregame rehearsal and follow it up with some pizza. Ask the basketball coach and the principal to stop by and welcome the middle school students.

- **Organize a monthly checklist for recruiting students from the middle school to the high school.** Stick to it. Make the list specific with due dates and action items. The less time there is needed to think about what to do, the more time there is to accomplish these tasks.

- **Host a "Parent Night"** where the high school students teach the parents of the middle school students how to play while they demonstrate how worthwhile it is to be in the high school program. Once the parents have participated, give each parent a certificate making them an "Honorary Band Member."

- **Arrange for a "Switch Day"** where the high school directors switch with middle school directors and teach each other's classes. Be sure to "coach" students how to behave and encourage each one to personally speak to the visiting director and say "thank you."

- **Create a recruiting page from the high school band website that provides a variety of student photos.** Get the e-mail addresses of the middle school students and e-mail them blasts about your program on a regular basis. Consider using other social media such as Facebook or Twitter.

- **Work with the local paper and school newspaper/ publication to start a "Music Corner"** to publicize the many achievements and community events provided by the school's program—include photos. Approach local merchants who regularly advertise and ask them to devote a part of their ad to salute student achievement or to publicize an upcoming concert.

- **Use technology in programming to demonstrate the school's up-to-date program.** If uploading performances, be sure the excerpts are quality. Consider having a student introduce the video clip. Consider how to incorporate the use of technology into teaching as well as homework assignments.

- **Maintain high performance standards for students but be reasonable in demands on their time.** Do not overburden them to the point that being in the program takes an inordinate amount of time away from their other activities. Never put students in a position where they HAVE to quit the program because they just do not have the amount of time required to participate. Think of their participation in music as one of many subjects they are taking at school. When you do have extra rehearsals or activities, make sure that their time is never wasted. Always provide a meaningful experience.

- **Work with guidance counselors to guarantee that all students are scheduled appropriately.** Develop a formatted schedule for college-bound students that shows how they can continue to participate in the program while taking all of their required coursework. Find out what the course of study would be for those who want to be music majors. If students and parents can see a carefully planned out schedule that shows how they can continue to participate in music and still be accepted into college, they are more likely to remain in the program.

- **Make time to speak to the principal** to ensure that he/she understands that when music class is over, music students are dispersed throughout the school. With those students comes the self-discipline and sense of teamwork that is routinely found in a music classroom. The behavior and habits formed in the music classroom carry over to the entire school.

- **Ensure that students understand how much they are valued and how much they contribute to the overall ensemble as individuals.** Do not allow them to just quit. Remember, praise pays. Be specific in your praise of student behavior or performance. Personal messages, handwritten notes and phone calls to parents are but a few ways to recognize students.

Advocate for Music Education.
Go to: **www.supportmusic.com**

3

Bridging The Gap between Middle School and High School

What PARENTS Can Do...

Parents speaking to other parents provides a more candid snapshot of the benefits of participating in the high school instrumental music program.

High school parents can:

- **Create partnership opportunities to come together with middle school parents.** In the same way that the high school and middle school directors must work together to ensure seamless transition within the instrumental music program, parent leaders must do the same. High school parents can break down a number of barriers— including language barriers—so high school parent leaders should partner with the middle school parent leaders to reach out to all parents.

- **Offer assistance and expertise to the middle school parents** to energize their efforts and help ensure success in their activities. Because high school parents have been involved for a longer period, they have a longitudinal view of the program.

- **Host an "Informational Parent Night" for the middle school parents;** high school parents have their own, distinctive perspective from that of the director(s). Directors will naturally encourage students to continue to participate in the program, but high school parents can provide unique insights for prospective incoming parents.

- **Invite the parents of the eighth-graders who will be performing at "Marching Band Night" to the football game as guests.** In this way, middle school parents will see their students participating as a member of the high school band program. High school parents could host a meeting/reception for the eighth-grade parents while students are warming up prior to the game. This will provide an inviting, casual opportunity for parents to speak openly to each other about the program. Involve the parents of the eighth-grade students as soon as possible so that they become engaged in the program.

- **Share experiences by mentoring eighth-grade parents individually so that open lines of communication may be established as early as possible.** The job of the mentoring parent is to address all concerns of the eighth-grade parent and ensure continued participation of the student. It can even go as far as like instrument mentoring— high school flute parents with middle school flute parents, for example.

- **Extend personal invitations to the assigned eighth-grade parents to attend and bring their students to the high school performances.** The parents that already have a band student in high school in addition to one in middle school can be especially effective in showing the importance of continuing on to the high school program.

4

- **Offer to host some of the middle school parent meetings in the high school facilities.** The more that middle school parents see themselves in the high school, the more obvious it becomes that instrumental music is a program that continues beyond the immediate level.

- **Prepare a dinner or potluck supper for the middle school students and their parents** just before a joint concert or create a special awards dinner for both middle school and high school students.

Advocate for Music Education.
Go to: **www.supportmusic.com**

5

Bridging The Gap between Middle School and High School

What STUDENTS Can Do...

High school instrumental students should serve as positive role models and present themselves as members of a student-centered program that middle school students would want to participate in throughout high school.

High school students can:

- **Serve as intern instructors in the free "Summer Lesson Program" for beginning students.** The high school students would benefit immeasurably from this type of peer coaching and the beginners would soon view these high school students as role models.

- **Offer to teach group lessons during the year or even assist with tutoring in a supervised setting.** High school seniors could sit in on rehearsals at the middle schools to provide musical leadership in the various sections.

- **Participate actively in all recruitment activities and performances.** High school students serve as the best public relations for the program because they provide their own unique perspective to its value. They can thus be positioned to demonstrate their acquired leadership skills by serving active roles in all aspects of the program. These students should be featured prominently.

- **Remain engaged in a substantive manner in the middle school program they came from** because this demonstrates overtly that instrumental music reaches beyond the middle school years. Speak to students and parents from their former middle school about the advantages—both short-term and long-term—of active participation in instrumental music. Offer to serve as emcee for the middle school concerts or other appropriate events.

- **Provide testimonials that show how participation in additional activities such as sports, cheerleading, drama, debate, etc., is possible.** A photo of a football player in uniform holding his trombone sends a great message that students can participate in music along with other activities. Speak with other students who may have objections to staying in the program and guide them in how it can be accomplished—especially with regard to scheduling. A short speech or presentation at the beginning of a rehearsal period can help greatly. Any objections the high school student can address while the prospective student is still in eighth grade will provide a better chance of keeping that student than trying reverse the decision to drop the program once it has already been made.

Want more tips for keeping music strong in your schools?
Go to: **www.supportmusic.com**

Bridging The Gap between Middle School and High School

What MUSIC SUPERVISORS Can Do...

Music supervisors represent and facilitate all aspects of the district-wide music program. In this capacity, the supervisor plays a critical role by serving as the link between and among all constituencies and decision-makers. Effective recruitment and retention is of paramount importance, and visionary leaders can assist directors in this process by aligning efforts and resources to ensure that all entities are working together to achieve the highest possible rate of continued participation.

All school music supervisors can:

- **Provide leadership with regard to district-wide vision, rationale, advocacy and communication.**

- **Work with site administrators to guide them in how they might assist in the recruitment and retention process.** Among other areas, this could include appropriate curriculum, scheduling, staffing, materials, equipment and facilities.

- **Track transitional enrollment and participation data at all district facilities/ programs to ensure articulation.**

- **Provide sample schedules that reflect how students can continue to participate while in the college prep (or other) track.**

- **Ensure that music educators are provided with the essential information to facilitate continued enrollment.** Among other items, this could include publications (tri-folds) about the district-wide music program, student achievement and a website that is open to the community that features district-wide programs and/or students.

- **Provide additional opportunities (Honor Ensembles, Solo & Ensemble Festivals) for students to continue their involvement in music.**

- **Provide professional development opportunities for music educators.**

Advocate for Music Education.
Go to: **www.supportmusic.com**

7

Bridging The Gap between Middle School and High School

What PRINCIPALS Can Do...

Principals of high schools or middle schools with large and active music programs will tell you that these programs make a significant impact in the achievement level of the student body and contribute positively to the overall environment of their campuses. Principals thus have a vested interest in ensuring continued, successful participation of the middle school students in the high school program. Directors may need to foster an awareness of the benefits of continued participation yet it is worth it to have an influential ally in this area.

High school principals can:

- **Work with middle school principal(s) to facilitate cooperative recruitment assemblies/events/programs at the middle school(s).**

- **Work with middle school principals to ensure appropriate scheduling** so that directors from both levels may work cooperatively to best benefit each other's students.

- **Demonstrate their collaboration with and support for middle school principals and vice versa by creating a joint presentation for the middle school band parents,** speaking to the value of continued participation in the instrumental music program beyond the intermediate level.

- **Invite middle school principals to provide "opening remarks" at any of the concerts hosted at the high school that involve former middle school students.** In this way, current middle school students and their parents readily see that their principal is an advocate for the high school program. In addition, middle school principals are provided with an opportunity to see former students engaged in a successful program—something which he/she had a hand in providing.

Resources

Music Achievement Council Resources available

- A Practical Guide for Recruitment and Retention (with CD)

- Tips for Success 24 Different Topics

- First Performance for Beginning Instrumental Music Students
  - Band
  - Orchestra

The Music Achievement Council Website was designed to provide instrumental music teachers with materials, tips, tools and resources to support their goal of recruiting and retaining students.

Tips for Success will help answer a range of questions, from how to prepare an instrument replacement plan to how to expand the learning power of music. These tips are complemented by short videos and will enhance the user's experience.

This Web Site section also features products that teachers can order or download for use in their classrooms. Sample marketing letters, actions that help retain students and information on how to get parents involved are all provided in the **Practical Guide for Recruitment and Retention.**

Music Education Advocacy Websites:

- Support Music Coalition
  http://www.nammfoundation.org/support-music

- Music Advocacy Groundswell
  http://advocacy.nafme.org/

- ArtsEdSearch
  http://www.artsedsearch.org/

- Americans for the Arts
  http://www.americansforthearts.org/get_involved/advocate.asp

- Music For All
  http://www.musicforall.org/

Advocate for Music Education.
Go to: **www.supportmusic.com**

9

Bridging The Gap between Middle School and High School